Raging Reptiles!

GROOVY TUBE BOOK™

written by **JAN JENNER**
illustrated by **BERNARD ADNET**

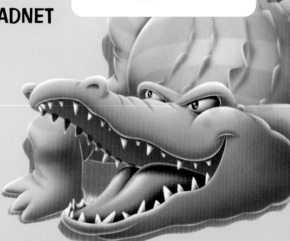

Line art by Roseanne Kakos-Main
Game by Eric Berlin

PHOTO CREDITS
P. 9 (top): Herb Segars Photography; p. 16: John Sullivan/Ribbit Photography;
p. 22: Frans Lanting, copyright © 2004

Conceived, developed, and designed by the creative team at innovativeKids®.
Copyright © 2004 by innovativeKids®
All rights reserved
Published by innovativeKids®, a division of innovative USA®, Inc.
18 Ann Street, Norwalk, CT 06854
iKids is a registered trademark in Canada and Australia.
ISBN: 978-1-58476-268-3
20 19 18 17 16 15 14 13 12 11 10

Not for individual sale

ZAP!
You're a Reptile!

If you were a reptile, you might have a long scaly tail or a shell that makes you into a walking armored tank. Your skin might even change color to match your surroundings. No matter what, you wouldn't be able to walk upright—reptiles can only creep, crawl, slither, or glide. And you'd probably live in a dangerous environment—a swamp or the hot, hot desert. Being a reptile is hard work!

Leaping Lizards!

There are more lizards than any other kind of reptile—4,450 different kinds. Most lizards are very small. One lizard, the dwarf lizard, is so tiny that an adult can fit on a dime! These smaller lizards tend to eat plants and insects. The largest living lizard is the Komodo dragon. This giant can grow up to 9 feet long and weigh over 440 pounds. A Komodo dragon attacks its prey with one bite—and then waits. Over the next few days, poisonous bacteria from its mouth slowly kill the prey. The Komodo tracks down the dying prey by "smelling" with its tongue.

The Komodo dragon is the largest lizard.

The chameleon is a medium-sized lizard. It snares prey by shooting out its sticky tongue to twice the length of its body! Chameleons' eyes are amazing, too. To enlarge what they see, the eyes have zoom lenses! As if this weren't enough, a chameleon can move its left and right eyes independently. One eye can watch a bug while the other looks out for predators.

A chameleon looks for bugs.

Scaly Secrets

Most of the time, basilisk lizards walk on four legs like other lizards do. But when a basilisk is trying to escape from a predator, it stands up on its hind legs and runs! A basilisk can even run for a short distance across the surface of water.

What a Croc!

Crocodiles, alligators, caimans, and gavials are their own group of reptiles called crocodilians. Crocs have thick skulls and teeth that are set into sockets to give them a firm grip on struggling prey. Crocs are ferocious and mighty predators! When they get hungry, they attack and eat nearly anything they can get.

Crocodilians make more noise than other reptiles. When a male American alligator has chosen where he wants to live, he defends his territory with a bellowing sound and chases away other males.

Nile crocodiles live crowded together on muddy shorelines. If a larger male comes along, a smaller croc may save his own life by lifting his chin, a gesture that shows he knows who's the boss.

A crocodile basking in the sun

A gavial glides through the water.

Gavials have long, narrow snouts full of razor-sharp teeth. A gavial's snout looks needle-nosed when compared to the broader snouts of crocodiles, alligators, or the smaller caiman. The gavial's narrow snout causes less movement in the water, allowing it to slide underwater and sneak up on schools of fish.

Scaly Secrets

Today's crocs are shorties in comparison with their relatives from long, long ago. The Nile crocodile grows to about 20 feet long, but back in the Age of Dinosaurs, a crocodile might be 40 feet long—with a 6-foot-long skull!

Life in a Shell

A turtle or tortoise lives its whole life in a shell—made of bone! Large scales cover the box turtle's bony shell, and smaller scales cover its head, legs, and tail. Many turtles can pull their heads, legs, and tails into their shells when they feel threatened. Turtles and tortoises have sharp beaks instead of teeth.

A soft-shelled turtle buries itself in soft, sandy river bottoms and waits for unsuspecting fish to swim within range of its long and speedy neck. When something gets close, it snaps up a tasty little meal! Softshells have such flat shells that they look like leather pancakes.

A soft-shelled turtle peeks from its shell.

Scaly Secrets

What's the difference between a turtle and a tortoise? Turtles are adapted, or specially made, for water. They have broad, webbed feet and sleek, streamlined shells. Tortoises are adapted for life on land. They have stumpy feet and high, domed shells.

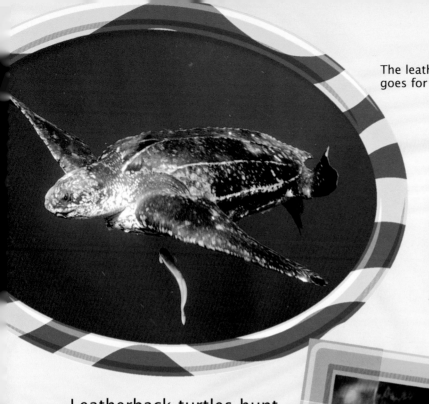

The leatherback turtle goes for a swim.

Galapagos giant tortoises are the longest-living vertebrates, or animals with backbones. They can weigh as much as 600 pounds and have shells that grow to 4 feet across. Just try to put one in a fishbowl!

A Galapagos tortoise can live over 100 years!

Leatherback turtles hunt jellyfish. Their sharp beaks pierce the jellyfishes' soft bodies, while their tough leathery shells protect against jellyfish stings. Leatherbacks are the largest turtles living— one of the largest weighed 1,900 pounds!

Sssssnakes Alive!

Snakes are lizards' closest relatives. The big difference between snakes and lizards is that snakes don't have legs. Instead of walking, snakes slither. Snakes also have stretchy skin and expandable jaws that can open very wide. This ability to expand their jaws and bodies is important because snakes are carnivores that swallow prey whole.

Snakes catch and kill prey in many ways. Constrictor snakes like the anaconda wrap their bodies around their prey and slowly squeeze. Each time the prey lets out its breath, the constrictor squeezes tighter. When the prey dies, the snake can eat it safely. A 25-foot-long anaconda once captured and swallowed a 100-pound pig.

Don't let the anaconda grab you!

A python can go months without eating.

False vipers eat toads that puff up to make themselves hard to swallow. These snakes use thick fangs in the back of their mouths to "pop" the toads!

The largest recorded meal for a snake was eaten by another constrictor: A 16-foot African python swallowed a 132-pound impala (a kind of antelope)!

Snakes have other ways of getting prey, too. The snail-eating snake has long teeth for prying snails out of their shells.

Scaly Secrets

If you were a snake, every now and then you would shed your entire skin. Shedding skin lets snakes grow bigger. Young snakes shed their skin more often than adults do, since they are growing more quickly.

Venomous sSSnakeSSS!

Some snakes have *venom*—a poison they inject into prey by biting them. Venom can be used to get rid of enemies, but venomous snakes would rather just scare their enemies away!

Rattlesnakes shake the rattles on their tails as a warning to enemies to get far away. You should always listen when a rattlesnake sends you a warning—its venom is highly poisonous to humans!

A rattlesnake warns its enemies.

Scaly Secrets

Snakes are not the only venomous reptiles. Gila monsters and Mexican beaded lizards also inject venom into their prey when they bite. These slow-moving lizards seldom bite humans—and you sure don't want to give them a reason to.

Cobras chase away enemies by lifting their heads and spreading their necks into hoods, making them look bigger. Then they sway back and forth before striking. When cobras bite, the venom leaves the victim unable to move. Then, it's time for lunch!

Venom helps snakes in another way, too. Snake venom often breaks down the prey, so that it can be eaten easily. This is important for the sea snake, which eats fish whole. A sea snake doesn't want to get poked by the sharp fins of its squirming, spiny meal!

This cobra is sending a warning!

A sea snake looks for fish to eat.

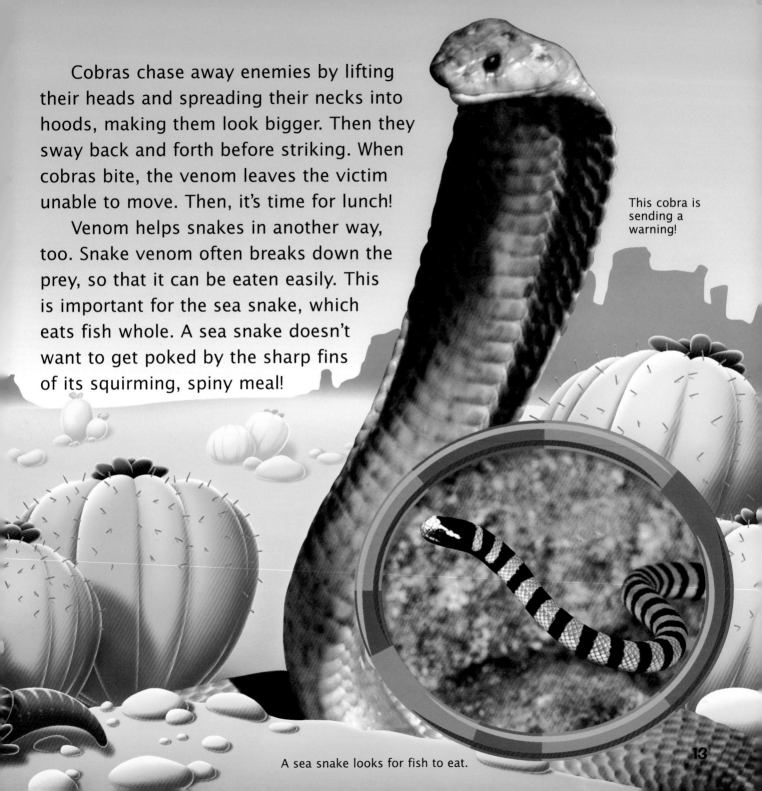

A baby turtle breaks out of its egg.

Here Comes Baby!

Most reptiles lay eggs. Some lay one egg at a time; others lay up to a hundred in one big clutch. Inside each egg, an embryo—a developing baby—floats in a pool of liquid, growing into a mini-version of its parents. A tough shell protects the egg from drying out. These shells are like leather, not brittle and chalky like the shells of chicken eggs.

A few reptiles lay a different kind of egg. Rattlesnakes and water snakes have eggs with filmy shells. These eggs are kept inside the mother's body. After the embryos have grown to be full-size hatchling snakes, the mother lays her eggs. Right away, the young snakes slash free of the filmy eggshells and slither their way into the world.

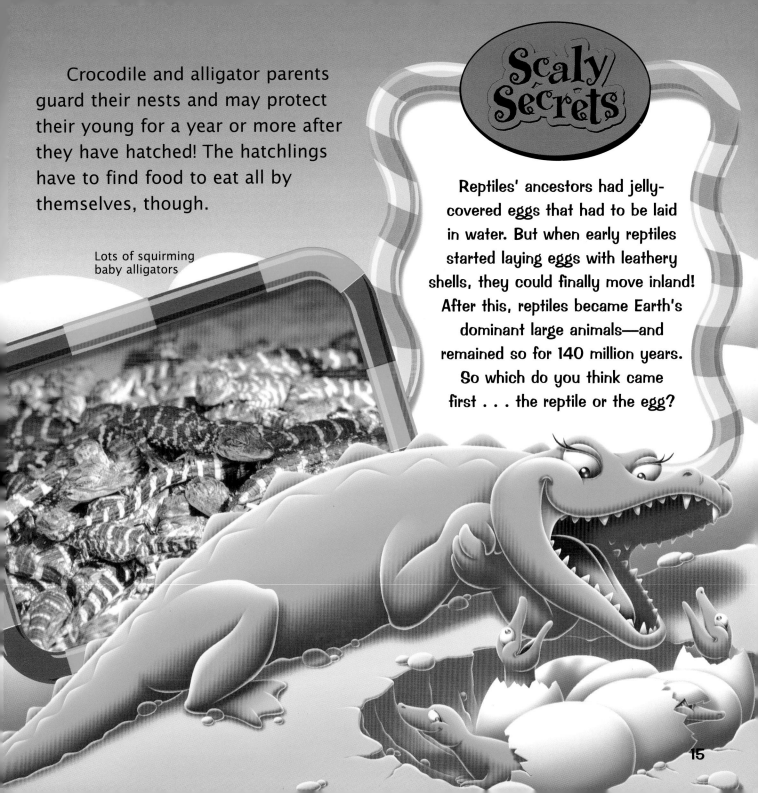

Crocodile and alligator parents guard their nests and may protect their young for a year or more after they have hatched! The hatchlings have to find food to eat all by themselves, though.

Lots of squirming baby alligators

Life in the Slow Lane

Reptiles are *cold-blooded*—their bodies do not heat up on their own. If a reptile can't warm up, its heartbeat, breathing, and other body functions slow down. If a reptile gets too cold, it might even die! That's why most reptiles live in hot places. The flying dragon spends its life in the steamy canopy of the tropical rainforest. To get away from predators, it just spreads out its ribbed "wings" and rides on the air like a paper airplane.

The flying dragon lives in the trees.

Scaly Secrets

A healthy human's heart beats about 72 times in one minute. But reptiles are really different. Their bodies run much more s-l-o-w-l-y. If you took the pulse of a reptile, you might count just ten heartbeats in a minute!

A Texas tortoise
may live 60 years.

Some reptiles do live in temperate climates where it's cold for part of the year. To cope with freezing weather, they hide out somewhere warm. Reptiles like rattlesnakes and Texas tortoises seek shelter in underground dens in autumn when the cold weather starts. During the winter, these reptiles hibernate, staying inactive. Their body temperatures fall and their body functions slow down to save energy. They don't come out until springtime, when the weather is warm again. Then they shed their skins, hunt for food and mates, and sunbathe.

17

A sidewinder's scales help it survive.

No Sweat!

Reptiles thrive in wet places like the rainforest, but they are also experts at surviving in the hot, dry desert. A desert reptile's body is built to save water. The sidewinder, for instance, has a layer of dry scales over its skin so that it doesn't lose water through its skin the way humans do.

To save still more water, reptiles do not sweat. When humans sweat, they are using water from their bodies to cool themselves off. Reptiles keep themselves cool by hiding in the shade.

Reptiles do not use liquid urine to get rid of body waste. Instead, many reptiles make a dry urine that looks like bird droppings. The white part of the dropping is the reptile's dry urine.

Reptiles that live in hot, dry places can overheat. To prevent this, some lizards, like the desert spiny lizard, pant, or breathe heavily, just like dogs do. Desert spinys also like to hide in cool, underground burrows during the hottest parts of the day. At especially hot times, many desert reptiles lie perfectly still and do nothing while hiding out somewhere cool.

When a desert reptile is active during the day, it can move in ways that keep it from touching the hot sand. Lizards run on the tips of their claws, holding their bodies high up on their legs. Just imagine running around on the tips of your toenails!

Below: The Galápagos by Corel.
†390ᵖ Galápagos 9

A desert spiny takes a break.

19

Don't Mess with Me

Many reptiles do interesting things when they are in danger. If the male anole lizard finds another male anole in his territory, he lifts his chin, puffs out a pouch of brightly colored skin, and bobs his head. In response, the other anole may do the same thing. This contest is won when one anole attacks the other.

The hognose snake will roll over and play dead when in danger. If you turn it back over, it will turn over again, as if saying, "I'm dead! Really, I'm dead!" The hognose does this because many predators will lose interest in a dead animal.

An anole puffs up to scare an enemy.

Other reptiles try to scare away their enemies. A frilled lizard will stiffen its cape of brightly colored skin, turning it into a wide collar around its open and hissing jaw. Like an umbrella that is suddenly opened, the collar makes the small lizard look much bigger.

A frilled lizard makes itself look bigger.

Scaly Secrets

Alligator snapping turtles often lie perfectly still underwater on a riverbed, with their mouths open. Their tongue looks just like a little pink worm! When a fish swims up to eat the delicious-looking worm, the turtle snaps its jaws shut and gulps down a fishy snack.

Reptile Roots!

Those amazing tuataras may look like lizards but they are really the only surviving species of an ancient group of early reptiles called beakheads. Tuataras can live to be 100 years old. And they can hold their breath for as long as an hour. A tuatara will share a burrow with birds, but it might bite off a baby bird's head if it is hungry!

Fossils show that tuataras haven't changed much in 225 million years! Fossils are traces of life preserved in rock. Fossils show that prehistoric reptiles ruled the planet 65 to 200 million years ago!

Tuataras can live for 100 years.

Scaly Secrets

Tuataras have three eyes! The third eye is a small, light-sensitive eye that sits right in the middle of its forehead.

While dinosaurs are considered reptiles, fossils show that there were other reptiles alive even before the dinos existed! Modern crocodiles have been around for about 100 million years. Snakes appeared around the same time. Turtles are even older—they date back 250 million years and are still going strong! These raging reptiles have been around for a long, long time! And if we humans are careful and protect their environments, reptiles will be an important part of our amazing and sometimes downright weird world of nature for a very long time to come.

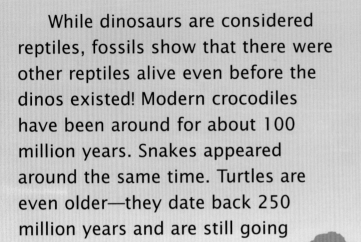

The fossilized jaw of a crocodile

MORE

Scaly Secrets

DROP THAT TAIL

If a predator grabs the tail of a gecko, the tail might suddenly drop off! The tail will continue to wriggle, making the predator think its caught a meal. Meanwhile, the gecko makes a dash up the nearest tree. A new tail will slowly grow back over time.

HEY, SQUIRT!

Horned toads, which are actually lizards, have an unusual way of scaring away their enemies—they hiss, puff up their bodies, and squirt blood from the corners of their eyes!

LOST: ONE TOOTH

A reptile baby gets out of its egg by cutting an escape hatch using the sharp "egg tooth" on its snout. Soon after it crawls free of the eggshell, the egg tooth falls off.

STUCK ON YOU

The chameleon can shoot its sticky tongue out to twice the length of its body. If you had a tongue like a chameleon and were 3 feet tall, your tongue would be 6 feet long (and as sticky as glue)!